Hospitality

Look for these topics in the
Everyday Matters Bible Studies for Women

Acceptance	Mentoring
Bible Study & Meditation	Outreach
Celebration	Prayer
Community	Reconciliation
Confession	Sabbath & Rest
Contemplation	Service
Faith	Silence
Fasting	Simplicity
Forgiveness	Solitude
Gratitude	Stewardship
Hospitality	Submission
Justice	Worship

Hospitality

Spiritual Practices
FOR EVERYDAY LIFE

HENDRICKSON
PUBLISHERS

Everyday Matters Bible Studies for Women—Hospitality

@ 2013 by Hendrickson Publishers Marketing, LLC
P.O. Box 3473
Peabody, Massachusetts 01961-3473

ISBN 978-1-61970-169-4

Unless otherwise noted, all Scripture references are taken from the *Everyday Matters Bible for Women*, New Living Translation. Copyright © 1996, 2004, 2007 by Tyndale House Foundation. Used by permssion of Tyndale House Publishers, Inc., Carol Stream, Illinois 60188. All rights reserved.

Printed in the United States of America

First Printing — November 2013

Contents

Holy Habits

Spiritual Practices for Everyday Life

Everyday life today is busier and more distracting than it has ever been before. While cell phones and texting make it easier to keep track of children and each other, they also make it harder to get away from the demands that overwhelm us. Time, it seems, is a shrinking commodity. But God, the Creator of time, has given us the keys to leading a life that may be challenging but not overwhelming. In fact, he offers us tools to do what seems impossible and come away refreshed and renewed. These tools are called spiritual practices, or spiritual disciplines.

Spiritual practices are holy habits. They are rooted in God's word, and they go back to creation itself. God has hardwired us to thrive when we obey him, even when it seems like his instructions defy our "common sense." When we engage in the holy habits that God has ordained, time takes on a new dimension. What seems impossible is actually easy; it's easy because we are tapping into God's resources.

The holy habits that we call spiritual practices are all geared to position us in a place where we can allow the Holy Spirit to work in us and through us, to grant us power and strength to do the things we can't do on our own. They take us to a place where we can become intimate with God.

While holy habits and everyday life may sound like opposites, they really aren't. As you learn to incorporate spiritual practices into your life, you'll find that everyday life is easier. At the same time, you will draw closer to God and come to a place where you can luxuriate in his rich blessings. Here is a simple example. Elizabeth Collings hated running household errands. Picking up dry cleaning, doing the grocery shopping, and chauffeuring her kids felt like a never-ending litany of menial chores. One day she had a simple realization that changed her life. That day she began to use her "chore time" as a time of prayer and fellowship with God.

Whenever Elizabeth walked the aisle of the supermarket, she prayed for each person who would eat the item of food she selected. On her way to pick up her children, she would lay their lives out before God, asking him to be there for them even when she couldn't. Each errand became an opportunity for fellowship with God. The chore that had been so tedious became a precious part of her routine that she cherished.

The purpose of these study guides is to help you use spiritual practices to make your own life richer, fuller, and deeper. The series includes twenty-four spiritual practices that are the building blocks of Christian spiritual formation. Each practice is a "holy habit" that has been modeled for us in the Bible. The practices are acceptance, Bible study and meditation, celebration, community, confession, contemplation, faith, fasting, forgiveness, gratitude, hospitality, justice, mentoring, outreach, prayer, reconciliation, Sabbath and rest, service, silence, simplicity, solitude, stewardship, submission, and worship.

As you move through the practices that you select, remember Christ's promise in Matthew 11:28–30:

> *Come to me, all of you who are weary and carry heavy*
> *burdens. Take my yoke upon you. Let me teach you, because*
> *I am humble and gentle at heart, and you will find rest for*
> *your souls. For my yoke is easy to bear, and the burden I give*
> *you is light.*

Introduction

to the Practice of Hospitality

Out of God's abundance we are called to share and live lives of welcoming hospitality. Michelle Hershberger sums up biblical hospitality in her reflection in the *Everyday Matters Bible for Women*. "Hospitality, in a sense, is being willing to see Christ in others," she says. "It's the intentional practice of putting yourself in a situation to both receive Christ in others and extend Christ's love to others."

So we turn from the limited ideal that has been planted in our minds through magazines, websites, and shows with home decorating and chef superstars—which make our attempts seem inadequate—to the unlimited richness of Christ's example. From his outpouring our lives overflow. And what is offered to God, even the simplest gift, can be used in amazing ways.

The discipline of hospitality prompts us to ask, "What does love look like?" God answers that question through us as we serve others and embrace our neighbor as ourselves. As God welcomes us, we are called to welcome others in his name. Hospitality takes on the shape of the one served. It is not one-size-fits-all. There is a world full of expressions of hospitality, and they all come back to the basic need to be treated as family, to see the reality of who we are in Christ, related in the kingdom.

The spiritual discipline of hospitality focuses us on what is important—what will last. The truth is that in a world of things, people matter more. And so we open our eyes. We practice seeing the people around us. And God helps us to see the ones we might walk past—the ones we might ignore.

Through the study of Scripture, we go deeper into our relationship with Christ and into finding out the ways our calling can come to be reflected in everything we do. God wants us to live a life of "power, love and self-discipline," using all that we are for his glory (2 Timothy 1:7)—heart, soul, mind, and strength all given over to serve his purpose, inviting others to experience his grace.

CHAPTER 1

Divine Invitation

Lives of Welcome & Grace

How precious is your unfailing love, O God! All
humanity finds shelter in the shadow of your
wings. You feed them from the abundance
of your own house, letting them drink
from your river of delights. For you are the
fountain of life, the light by which we see.

PSALM 36:7-9

---

*For this study, read Leviticus 19:33–34
and Deuteronomy 10:17–19.*

It seems like just when the only thing left in the refrigerator
is growing green fuzz, just when the house is at its messiest,
just when we couldn't possibly squeeze one more thing onto
our already full calendars, along comes an opportunity to
practice hospitality. God doesn't wait for us to have everything fixed and perfect. God shows up. He invites us with
his grace to live out hospitality in spite of our messy reality.
He is the source, and this is where we start. Right here in
the middle of where we are.

The Psalms show us how we have been invited through God's generous hospitality: "All humanity finds shelter in the shadow of your wings." And we see time and again in Scripture that God's welcome doesn't wear out. As the psalmist reminds us, "Your unfailing love, O Lord, is as vast as the heavens; your faithfulness reaches beyond the clouds" (Psalm 36:5).

When God is the source, he can take even everyday things and transform them. It didn't seem like much, just wafers on the ground. The people had complained, and God heard their grunts and groans and provided food. A little boy offered bread and fish. Jesus broke bread and offered wine. Whether it's a wedding feast or a crowd of hungry mouths to feed, what God touches, he transforms. From something simple with his lavish presence he invites us. And we are never the same. God transforms us by his grace. "For in him we live and move and exist" (Acts 17:28).

We start with who God is—love, flowing out in expressions of care. As we seek to reflect that servant heart, we then start with who we are: people whose lives aren't perfect and are often complicated, sinners transformed by God's grace, called to live transforming lives. We begin with what we have and God multiplies it and magnifies it for his glory.

The psalmist gives an account in stark contrast to a life of sin: "Sin whispers to the wicked, deep within their hearts" (Psalm 36:1). God calls us deeper with shouts and songs. His love is not silent.

At a banquet feast, water is turned into wine. The best is saved for last. God welcomes us with his divine invitation. God's grace fills us with enough. We come back to the source. We offer God gratitude or grunts and complaints. But however we respond, God's faithfulness is still the same. His love invites us and propels us to do the same for others. Hospitality is woven into the fabric of his being. Who God is gives us strength to be who he called us to be. And because we are his, we have more than enough to give.

Hospitality is a discipline that transforms not only us, but others as well. God's love is the source of our strength and action. "For you are the fountain of life, the light by which we see" (Psalm 36:9). From being known, we seek to know others. From being seen, we seek to see others as Jesus sees them.

When the source of our everyday lives gets overlooked, hospitality becomes a struggle or gets pushed further down the to-do list. But the discipline of hospitality is rooted in joy, not duty. It is not a burden but a blessing when we rightly see that "you feed them from the abundance of your own house" (Psalm 36:8).

A place of abundance is where God is. We are welcomed each day to live in God's embrace in fullness and hope so that we can extend them to others. God's gaze transforms even a dirt-floored shack into a palace of his Spirit. He turns our emptiness into jars overflowing with oil. A closed fist is opened through his welcoming forgiveness.

It doesn't seem like much, just some soup and saltines for a sick coworker. Throwing the surprise birthday party a friend thought she would never receive. Visiting a man in hospice whose only relatives live hours away. It isn't much. But it is enough. More than enough for God to transform for his glory.

Each day, no matter what the day brings, God is there to greet us and help us to live lives of welcome and grace.

> **As you study this chapter, reflect on how you have practiced hospitality in the past.**

1. What has been your definition of hospitality and how has it matched your actions? How does looking at God's grace refine your definition? How does God's grace transform our practice?

2. In Psalm 36 we hear the words of David, "a servant of the Lord." He was imperfect like the rest of us—in fact, the Bible gives dramatic accounts of his ups and downs. But even when he failed he turned back to God's "unfailing love" (36:5). How do our failings help us in offering hospitality that is genuine? What part does forgiveness play in hospitality?

3. We often live out of a sense of what we lack instead of seeing God's unlimited resources and the abundance that surrounds us. Jesus said, "My purpose is to give them a rich and satisfying life" (John 10:10). How does hospitality remind us of what is important? Do I live a life of half empty or half full? What are some ways I can live in gratitude and shift my focus?

4. God invites us into communion with him. This is fully expressed in Christ whose life embodies hospitality. In *Life Together*, Dietrich Bonhoeffer writes, "He [Christ] is the true bread of life. He is not only the giver but the gift itself." How do we see throughout Scripture God as the source and the substance of hospitality?

5. God uses his creativity to provide for his people, and David centers on God through poetry and song. What creative ways can you use your gifts in offering hospitality?

6. In her reflection in the *Everyday Matters Bible for Women,* "Accepting God's Hospitality," Michele Hershberger found an important truth about the practice of hospitality: "I've discovered it ultimately begins with opening myself to receive God's hospitality." What are some ways you receive God's hospitality?

7. As you explore the practice of hospitality, think about the other spiritual practices and how they relate to and impact each other. Some might seem a natural fit with hospitality, such as celebration, community, and service. How do prayer, simplicity, justice, or contemplation tie in to hospitality? What is another spiritual practice that would help in your practice of hospitality?

Points to Ponder

In Psalm 36, David's sweeping praise points to how all of creation is bound up in God's care.

- How does thankfulness connect us and fuel our generosity toward others? Instead of just making a list of things you are thankful for, find creative ways to live out this thankfulness.

- Are you thankful for friendship and the people who have offered welcome? Instead of jotting down your thoughts in another eloquent journal entry, write a note to someone or make a call.

- Are you thankful for the stars or that beautiful morning birdsong? Invite someone on a nature walk or share herbs from your garden. Take your gratitude with you.

The Psalms are filled with praise and examples of God's provision and hospitality. In Psalm 91, the psalmist proclaims, "He alone is my refuge, my place of safety." We like to think about hospitality in terms of positive events, but how can we help someone through a difficult time? What are some situations where you can provide refuge? What are some situations where you can point someone to a Christian organization able to handle their need? Make a list of contact information for area resources that provide services and loving hospitality for those in need.

"Grace is the hospitality of God to welcome sinners not because of their goodness but because of his glory." — John Piper

Sometimes we long for a simpler time when schedules were not so hectic and we didn't feel as fractured.

- How does our technologically connected world impact our practice of the discipline of hospitality?

- How does it make it easier for us to show hospitality? How does it make it harder?

Prayer

Lord, let us join with Paul when he says, "I pray that from his glorious, unlimited resources he will empower you with inner strength through his Spirit. Then Christ will make his home in your hearts as you trust in him. Your roots will grow down into God's love and keep you strong. And may you have the power to understand, as all God's people should, how wide, how long, how high, and how deep his love is. May you experience the love of Christ, though it is too great to understand fully. Then you will be made complete with all the fullness of life and power that comes from God. Now all glory to God, who is able, through his mighty power to work within us, to accomplish infinitely more than we might ask or think" (Ephesians 3:16–20).

Lord, your abundance and unfailing love still surprise us. We confess that we are often stuck selfishly thinking "If only . . ." and living in shallow waters instead of joyfully experiencing the abundance of your fountain of life. Thank you for making your home in our hearts and help us to live out your welcome in the world.

Add your prayer in your own words.

Amen.

Put It into Practice

This week, examine the cause of what keeps you from showing hospitality. What are the excuses that keep coming up?

Let God's benevolent gaze help you live out a life of hospitality for his glory.

Take-away Treasure

Hospitality is at the heart of who God is—the ultimate expression being God's love in Christ who embodied welcome. Take time to rest in God's love, to know the unlimited embrace of God's grace for you. No matter how simple our gifts seem, when they are offered to God, he can use it for his glory. "For God is working in you, giving you the power to do what pleases him" (Philippians 2:13).

CHAPTER 2

A Posture of Humility

Our Actions Are Arrows

Jesus replied, "'You must love the Lord your
God with all your heart, all your soul, and
all your mind.' This is the first and greatest
commandment. A second is equally important:
'Love your neighbor as yourself.'"

MATTHEW 22:37-39

For this study, read Luke 10:25–37.

In Luke 10 we meet a man who comes to Jesus with questions. But he knows the answers before he even asks. "Teacher, what should I do to inherit eternal life?" he asks Jesus. Jesus asks him to give the answer that he already knows: "'You must love the Lord your God with all your heart, all your soul, all your strength, and all your mind.' And 'Love your neighbor as yourself.'" In his exchange with Jesus, the man reveals a hidden truth about his life. He would rather be right and win a debate, than live rightly. He comes with hidden motives. He "wanted to justify his actions" and so he asks one more question. "And who is my neighbor?" This expert in religious law wanted to trick

Jesus, but he didn't realize that he was dealing with an expert too—an expert in the law of love.

Hospitality is how we answer with our actions this question of "Who is my neighbor?" We know the "shoulds": flossing, looking before we cross the street, saving for a rainy day. And sometimes hospitality just feels like another "should." But God doesn't want us to just cross things off our list. He wants to enlist us in a life of joyful service. To do this, he turns everything upside down—at least from our perspective. We find confusing truths that the last are first, the poor are rich, and in weakness there is strength. The focus shifts to him.

Our actions are arrows—that is, our lives point to something, often to ourselves. But God wants to show us how to turn our life toward him. How do we practice this discipline? Is the answer just more? Are we supposed to turn our homes into 24/7 hotels? Are we supposed to have a new person at every meal? Should we be a revolving door of food pantry and clothing distribution?

Hospitality is a discipline of discernment. You have probably seen people who have burnt out by extending so much of themselves that they had nothing left but bitterness. When God says he can use weakness does he want us to work to the point of burnout? What is healthy hospitality? Does being humble mean that I just see to it that others get what they ask for? When God gives us a heart for others, he helps us look for ways to meet needs they might not have even known they had. To look for lasting solutions, invest in real relationships. It's complicated. We can't solve everyone's problems in our own strength, and we aren't called to stay only on the surface.

Through the examples of others, I have seen what humble hospitality and loving my neighbor looks like. Serving recent immigrants has helped our family see how much even those who have very few possessions can offer through friendship and the joy of extending the invitation into their lives. On a visit to one family's small apartment, I was prepared as I entered the door to do my usual routine of complimenting the hosts on their home. I thought this was the nice thing to do. As we walked inside, I realized there wasn't much there in their sparse apartment. Struggling for words, a picture on the wall, one of the few things they brought from their country, caught my eye, and so I told my host how lovely it was. Her quick response caught me off guard. "You like it? It's yours." And she meant it. It took the whole rest of the visit to convince her not to send the picture home with us.

The thing of beauty, a prize possession, she was willing to give. Her words hit me, and I was humbled. I think I had thought about "what's mine is yours" in theory and it sounded nice. But what would I give up? Would I really give everything? What was I holding on to?

Humility brings us to our knees. We are on our knees in repentance. We are on our knees in praise. We are on our knees in service. But God exalts the smallest things and gives beauty to the simplest acts. We see differently from our knees. The life around us is bigger than we expected. We have been given more than we could have imagined. Grace fills in the gaps. Stress turns to surrender.

Jesus answers the man's question of who his neighbor is with a story. We see it in slow motion. A man attacked and bloody is left abandoned by the side of the road. Those who should have cared do not. But a man who has been abandoned by society—a Samaritan—stops, has compassion, and acts. The Samaritan saw. He felt. He went. We know the answers, but sometimes we would rather justify our actions than act justly.

The beauty of the big picture is that God takes a series of seemingly insignificant moments and turns them into something more. Again, we see it in slow motion. But it is not just a story. It is our story. It is the story of the way we have been cared for by one who was despised and rejected. It is the story of the God who loves us in real time. Every hour and every minute. Every precious second. And we can decide how to make the most beautiful picture from all the scenes we have a part in.

We don't always recognize the impact. We don't always see the fruits of our actions. From the ground sometimes it is hard to see all that God has done through a life of humble obedience, caring for others through hospitality, when it would have been easier to turn away to find an excuse to keep walking on alone.

Our actions are arrows. Who do we point to? Does our life create space for welcome and show others they are loved? Or is it just a big gleaming neon sign announcing our own amazingness? It's hard in this age of social media to not spew a constant stream of "Look at me!" Can God transform even our digital space to be a place of hospitality?

We are on the road. We are on the journey. Sometimes we know what it is like to be passed by, to be hurting and feel abandoned. Sometimes we have passed others by. We just didn't have the time or energy. But it is not our time and it is not our energy. When we are in Christ, our actions—even small ones—become arrows that lead others home. Once broken, now healed and whole.

> **As you consider these exercises, reflect on the attitude behind the actions.**

1. What does it mean to have the attitude of Christ? What does that look like in daily life? Why does it matter what our thoughts are as long as our actions are good?

2. God wants us to examine how we do what we do and not just what we do. In 2 Corinthians 9:7–8 Paul says, "You must each decide in your heart how much to give. And don't give reluctantly or in response to pressure. 'For God loves a person who gives cheerfully.' And God will generously provide all you need. Then you will always have everything you need and plenty left over to share with others." How does a discipline become more than just a have-to, but rather a joy?

3. Humility doesn't come from a lack of self-worth or putting ourselves down. People often deflect a compliment saying, "Oh, no, it's nothing . . ." or "It's no big deal." How could we turn the conversation toward Christ? True humility gives and appreciates thanks and points the praise to God. What are simple ways we can directly and indirectly acknowledge the source of our hospitality?

4. The example of the early believers is based on a humble heart. They "were united in heart and mind. And they felt that what they owned was not their own, so they shared everything they had" (Acts 4:32). In her reflection in the *Everyday Matters Bible for Women*, Marilyn Chandler McEntyre talks about a modern minister's wife whose generosity came from the recognition and attitude that "it's all God's stuff." How do we view our own lives and what we have in relation to others? What is easy to offer? What is difficult for us to give?

5. Romans 12:10 challenges us to "love each other with genuine affection, and take delight in honoring each other." This takes our actions a step deeper, not just to help but to honor. How can you honor others with your hospitality? How have you experienced being honored?

6. Jesus gave his disciples an example to follow as he washed their feet: "He loved them to the very end" (John 13:1). What are some other examples of Jesus' humble hospitality? How does Jesus challenge our view of hospitality beyond our comfort level?

7. Sometimes we think that someday we will practice hospitality when our lives are more presentable or everything is in place. How does humility help us see that God wants to use us where we are right now?

Points to Ponder

"And I know You move in greater ways/ But this is great enough for me/ What You do with my everyday is amazing," Sara Groves sings in "Everyday Miracles."

- How does God use the humble things in life to amaze us?

- Can you think of examples of the "everyday amazing"?

- How can inviting others into our lives and new perspective be a form of hospitality?

"Don't be selfish; don't try to impress others. Be humble, thinking of others as better than yourselves. Don't look out only for your own interests, but take an interest in others, too." (Philippians 2:3–4)

In Luke 3, John the Baptist gives the people examples of how to "produce good fruit": "If you have two shirts, give one to the poor. If you have food, share it with those who are hungry." And Jesus in Luke 6 takes it further with his challenge to love your enemies: "If someone demands your coat, offer your shirt also. Give to anyone who asks; and when things are taken away from you, don't try to get them back. Do to others as you would like them to do to you." How is sacrifice a part of hospitality?

"And so the first question that the priest asked, the first question that the Levite asked was, 'If I stop to help this man, what will happen to me?' But then the Good Samaritan came by, and he reversed the question: 'If I do not stop to help this man, what will happen to him?'"
— *Martin Luther King Jr. from his speech*
"I've Been to the Mountaintop," given April
3, 1968, the day before he was killed.

Prayer

Lord, you offered a perfect example of humble service. Help me to offer hospitality as a way to point to you and not feed my pride. Help me to know and love my neighbors and grow in empathy. As Saint Francis prayed, "God grant that I may not so much seek to be consoled, as to console; to be understood, as to understand; to be loved, as to love." Help me to put others first, becoming less and less to let you become greater so that my life might be filled with real joy.

Add your prayer in your own words.

Amen.

Put It into Practice

This week, choose someone to honor. Is there someone who goes unnoticed whom you could honor in a special way and help show that this person is loved and appreciated? Enlist the help of others and make it a group effort.

Take-away Treasure

We live anxiously, scattered by many concerns, but Christ focuses us on what matters. God brings us back to our knees, and in our weakness we experience his power and strength. We don't have to worry about inadequacies and our own failings; we can find freedom in his love and make a real difference in the lives of others instead of trying to impress them.

CHAPTER 3

Open Hearts & Hands

A Place at the Table

> " 'Go quickly into the streets and alleys of the
> town and invite the poor, the crippled, the blind
> and the lame.' After the servant had done this,
> he reported, 'There is still room for more.' "
>
> LUKE 14:21-23

For this study, read Luke 14:7–24.

The napkins have been folded into fans. The drinks have ice cubes with mint. The table name cards match the centerpieces, which match the invitations. It could be a magazine spread. It could be a Pinterest find. It's a masterpiece of color coordination and mood lighting. But it's definitely not everyone's life. This could be the place where we pause and think "someday" or it could be the place where we say "welcome."

The Bible doesn't often give us a detailed description of the setting and décor. We get a lot of close-up shots focused on people and relationships and interactions. In Luke's Gospel, Jesus eats a meal at the home of a leader of the Pharisees.

There is a man at the table with a "someday" attitude: "What a blessing it will be to attend a banquet in the Kingdom of God!" It seems a harmless statement, but Jesus reminds the man of the urgency of the kingdom work. Jesus tells the story of a great feast, where many invitations have been sent but only excuses roll in from the VIP guests.

Instead of trying to find a time to reschedule, the party thrower opens up the invitation: "Go quickly into the streets and alleys of the town and invite the poor, the crippled, the blind, and the lame." And when there is still more room, he says, "Go out into the country lanes and behind the hedges and urge anyone you find to come, so that the house will be full" (Luke 14:7–24).

Have we looked into the alleys and behind the hedges of our lives? Hospitality calls us further than our front door. It's easy to feel pity. But this is not a pity party that God has invited us to. From the distance of our own indifference, it's easy to forget the world around us. We have our clearly defined circle of friends. We have our families. We have our social life figured out. So much to care about already. God, do you really want me to invite even more into my life?

Hospitality is one way we help make God more visible in the world: "And as we live in God, our love grows more perfect" (1 John 4:17). The practice refines us and helps define what it means to be a Christ follower and what it means to live like Jesus.

The religious leaders asked pointedly in Mark 2:16, "Why does he eat with such scum?" When we see others through the eyes of faith, compassion springs our hearts and lives into action. Our attitude is changed. We can serve with purpose instead of just pity. We are motivated by love. We open our arms wider. Spread the net farther. Invite everyone. Make our hearts ready to receive him in fullness and joy. We are connected to others. Our circles aren't limited by our interests or the narrowness of our own needs. God sets the terms for engagement with the world.

Lydia is an example of a person who received the welcome of God washed in baptism and whose household was changed by faith. She eagerly invited the apostles as guests, saying, "Come and stay at my home" (Acts 16:15). God washed over her life with his love. He calls to us, "Come." Come and rest. Come and eat. Come and share in this joy. Come and be forgiven. Come and feast. Come and give.

Our hospitality allows others to be hospitable. When we share, it allows others to give. Our welcome reverberates in welcome. Love is never lost. When God's word dwells in us, it does not return empty. Empathy is never wasted.

When we look at our lives, who is on the guest list? Sometimes it's just a table for one. But how can we fill the table? The kingdom of God is never described as a single-size serving. It's a feast. It's a block party. Part of hospitality is remembering what and who we have to celebrate. Thankful lives are open. Thankful hearts are full and overflowing. Thankful hands serve. When we live in gratitude even simple things give cause for celebration.

Living in New York City can sometimes feel lonely even though you are often surrounded by people. In a recent street party, the community was celebrating and the open flow of guests invited others to join in. You couldn't help but be carried in by their joy. Spontaneity is part of hospitality.

There doesn't always have to be an engraved invitation—we carry our welcome mat with us. Even our body language and the words we use can express welcome or warning: "come in" or "keep out." The kettle is on or the door is closed. God reminds us that he is the one who provides and that there is always room for one more.

> *As you study this chapter, think about invitations you have received.*

1. Were there strings attached? Was there a dress code? Was there a hidden fee? How is hospitality different? What do we want people to take away from their experience?

2. God invites us to see with his eyes. How does God see us? God's love extends to the whole world. Revelation 22:17 gives a picture of God's invitation: "The Spirit and the bride say, 'Come.' Let anyone who hears this say, 'Come.' Let anyone who is thirsty come. Let anyone who desires drink freely from the water of life." What does it feel like to be invited and "come as you are"?

3. Sometimes our daily routines keep us stuck in the same small circle of concern. What are some things that keep us closed off to others? What are some little things we can change to make a big difference in how we see our neighbors, communities, and the world?

4. When we come together with other Christians we have more to share. How can we work with other believers? What are some ways our communities come together to offer hospitality? Brainstorm some ideas for extending hospitality as a community.

5. It might be easy to dismiss or ignore people based on our own preconceptions. When all we see are labels or stereotypes, how can we move from pity to true compassion?

6. In Colossians 2 Paul expresses his concern that believers continue to be connected to Christ: "Let your roots grow down into him, and let your lives be built on him." Our connection with Christ helps us to see how we are to be connected to others. How can we make sure that our efforts in hospitality are edifying and not just serving our own purposes?

7. How do we move beyond the surface? How does hospitality help us form and deepen relationships?

Points to Ponder

God doesn't play favorites. Deuteronomy 10 talks about how God "shows no partiality" and also "shows love to foreigners living among you and gives them food and clothing."

- How can you include and welcome others who might be newcomers and strangers?

- How do you talk about outsiders?

- Can you think of a time when you were a newcomer? How were you treated?

"Hospitality is the virtue which allows us to break through the narrowness of our own fears and to open our houses to the stranger, with the intuition that salvation comes to us in the form of a tired traveler. Hospitality makes anxious disciples into powerful witnesses, makes suspicious owners into generous givers, and makes close-minded sectarians into interested recipients of new ideas and insights."
— *Henri J. M. Nouwen,* Ministry and Spirituality

In her reflection in the *Everyday Matters Bible for Women* on the transformation of Lydia's life, Kelli B. Trujillo talks about how "Lydia's hospitality extended beyond Paul and Silas to encompass the entire new and growing Christian community in Philippi."

Sometimes we think of hospitality in terms of one-on-one or family-to-family, but how can we provide hospitality for groups and communities?

Prayer

Lord, thank you for extending your free invitation to the feast—a life of richness and joy that cannot be severed by circumstances. You call us to come and to welcome. You offer us a place at the table. Help me to offer that same welcome to the people in my life I have neglected and ignored. Help me to serve you with open arms that the whole world—person by person, family by family, community by community—might know and spread your salvation.

Add your prayer in your own words.

Amen.

"Therefore, accept each other as Christ has accepted you so that God will be given glory." (Romans 15:7)

Put It into Practice

Who are the strangers in your life?

This week, pray for them and ask God to show you how to be hospitable toward them.

Take-away Treasure

God's welcoming invitation reverberates his praise. God's hospitality is contagious. When he touches and transforms our life, we are liberated to love unconditionally and extend hospitality liberally. No one should be outside the reach of his open hands.

CHAPTER 4

Eternal Invitation

Living the Kingdom

"There is more than enough room in my Father's
home. If this were not so, would I have told you
that I am going to prepare a place for you? When
everything is ready, I will come and get you, so
that you will always be with me where I am."

JOHN 14:2-4

---

*For this study, read Acts 2:46–47 and 4:32–37,
Hebrews 13:1–3, and 1 Peter 4:7–11.*

This could have been their last meal together. Gathering
with Jesus at Passover, the disciples share a meal as Jesus
talks with them about who he is and who they are to be. He
serves them, washes their feet, and gives them a new commandment: "Love each other. Just as I have loved you, you
should love each other. Your love for one another will prove
to the world that you are my disciples" (John 13:34–35). He
tells them of the eternal welcome and the Father's home
that awaits them. But soon they would be tempted. Soon
they would be scattered. Soon Jesus would hang on a cross.

Soon Jesus would die. This could have been their last meal together, but the power of the gospel is that it was not.

On a beach Jesus shares a resurrection breakfast with his disciples. Again it is a simple meal, but something special is happening in the midst of the everyday. Miracles are happening all around them. Jesus gives them eyes to see. Out on a boat where an abundance of fish is being hauled in where only moments before there was nothing, Peter hears the voice of the Lord and heads for shore. Jesus welcomes Peter back with open arms and the challenge to "feed my lambs . . . take care of my sheep" (John 21:15–16). God resurrects relationships and he uses hospitality to show us his never-ending love.

Jesus turns this time together into an opportunity to build up what had been broken. To give sustaining love. To feed them so they can be nourished, ready to feed and nourish others. God's love is not an event; it is the invitation to life, living the kingdom.

The love of God propels us. Peter jumps out of the boat and finds forgiveness and serves the flock (John 21:7). Abraham runs to meet the guests "and welcomed them, bowing low to the ground" (Genesis 18:2). And the father "filled with love and compassion" runs to the prodigal son (Luke 15:20). God compels us to live out our calling with urgency.

Jesus shows us that the kingdom isn't limited. It keeps going and growing by his gracious hospitality. And Jesus reminds us that hospitality is not a one-time thing. "Keep on loving each other as brothers and sisters. Don't forget to show hospitality to strangers, for some who have done this have entertained angels without realizing it!" (Hebrews 13:1–2).

We make our New Year's resolutions—this year will be different, this time I'll be better. And then somewhere around mid-January we fizzle out. We get frustrated. We quit and move on. But our spiritual disciplines aren't like that. God is working in us, restoring us and helping us to see each opportunity, so that when something amazing happens we can say, "Look what God did!" We give him praise as our voices are joined by others. The sweet song of a life well lived in his service rises as we join others in the eternal chorus of the kingdom.

God comes back to us with welcome again and again. Sometimes it is not the first time we extend hospitality that is so powerful. Sometimes it is the second time or the seventy-seventh time. God does not release us from the circle of concern. Sometimes it is after we have been hurt that an unconditional invitation brings wholeness and peace.

Though we tend to think of hospitality in terms of our dwellings—the physical spaces we occupy—God shows us that he dwells in us: "The Spirit of God lives in you" (1 Corinthians 3:16). Hospitality doesn't stay on the surface but brings us into deeper relationships where God meets our deepest needs of acceptance, love, and forgiveness.

One day shortly after getting married, I was looking at the pretty journal we had used as a wedding guestbook, and saw all of the empty pages behind the names of those who attended. I wanted to find a way to use the pages and not . just shove the book on a shelf somewhere to be forgotten. I decided to use it as a guestbook, and over the years and many moves those who have stayed with us have written or drawn on the pages. We are blessed to be reminded of how

God uses guests to bless us with his presence. We give from our limitations only to be given from a God without limits. The book continues to help me remember a verse that we chose to remind us of the purpose of our life together, "Come, let us tell of the Lord's greatness; let us exalt his name together" (Psalm 34:3).

Jesus' welcome at that resurrection breakfast was a foretaste of the feast to come. He had already promised them an eternal welcome: "When everything is ready, I will come and get you, so that you will always be with me where I am" (John 14:3). And he promised the Holy Spirit as they waited for that kingdom to come. "He lives with you now and later will be in you. No, I will not abandon you as orphans" (John 14:17–18). God welcomes us as family, and we welcome others as the community of faith, as the people of God.

In the name of the Father and of the Son and of the Holy Spirit we have been welcomed and washed. Each day we begin in grace. With each word spoken in forgiveness and in love. With each "I can't do this." With each Hallelujah. Surrendering. Loving. Hoping. Caring. Offering our lives. We are fed to nourish others. The kingdom comes in us and through us. A life of blessing. A life of never-ending hospitality.

"Give as freely as you have received!" (Matthew 10:8)

> *As you study this chapter, think about what*
> *a lifetime of hospitality looks like.*

1. How will the discipline of hospitality look different through the different seasons of life? Be excited about what God will continue to do in and through you as you trust in and serve him.

2. God prepares a place for us. What part does preparation play in a life of hospitality? What steps can we take to make sure we are ready when an opportunity for invitation presents itself?

3. We are not just called to offer hospitality to those we like to be around. How does Jesus' example challenge us? How do we let our own pain or frustrations get in the way of offering hospitality?

4. In her reflection in the *Everyday Matters Bible for Women*, JoHannah Reardon talks about how, as an introvert, she offers hospitality even though her personality isn't geared toward being outgoing: "Hospitality will look different for introverts, but it can still be a powerful way God works in and through us." What are the things that make hospitality difficult for you? How can you be creative with what might seem like limitations?

5. Worship invites us into God's eternal celebration. Why do our churches sometimes seem like closed communities? How can we make our churches more welcoming?

6. Scripture offers us reminders of God's love and examples of how to live it. How can we place reminders in our lives that will point us to serving others with purpose? How do the choices of what we surround ourselves with affect our hospitality?

7. In 1 Peter 4:7–11, the apostle writes:

> *The end of the world is coming soon. . . . Most important of*
> *all, continue to show deep love for each other, for love covers*
> *a multitude of sins. Cheerfully share your home with those*
> *who need a meal or a place to stay. . . . Do you have the gift*
> *of helping others? Do it with all the strength and energy that*
> *God supplies. Then everything you do will bring glory to God*
> *through Jesus Christ.*

How does Peter impress on us the urgency of our calling?
How does this passage speak directly to you? How can you
bring glory to God?

We don't know how much time we have been gifted, but
how can we live with a sense of urgency without getting
stressed out? How do we set our priorities to focus on what
is important?

Points to Ponder

God's love was there before we were born, and God's love continues long after our last breath. We are invited to live out the love God has for us through hospitality. Hospitality helps others see their own worth and purpose.

- How can we demonstrate love across the span of life to show each person, young and old, to show that they are known and valued by God?

- How does hospitality help us see people differently?

In 1 Corinthians 10:27–31, Paul invites believers to accept hospitality from nonbelievers: "If someone who isn't a believer asks you home for dinner, accept the invitation if you want to. Eat whatever is offered to you without raising questions of conscience." This was a radical departure from past practices. Instead of feeling proud for distinguishing themselves from others, God called the people to live for his glory. "So whether you eat or drink, or whatever you do, do it all for the glory of God."

- What are some ways we can we show God's love when we accept the invitation of hospitality from others?

- How can we be good guests?

"'Come, you who are blessed by my Father, inherit the Kingdom prepared for you from the creation of the world. For I was hungry, and you fed me. I was thirsty and you gave me a drink. I was a stranger, and you invited me into your home. I was naked, and you gave me clothing. I was sick, and you cared for me. I was in prison, and you visited me. . . . When you did it to one of the least of these my brothers and sisters, you were doing it to me!'" (Matthew 25:34, 40)

Prayer

Lord, your love continues to be poured out into our lives. You welcome us and continue to welcome us back even when we turn away. We thank you for your eternal hospitality and the place you have prepared for us. Help us to follow your example and give us the strength and energy to serve you. Help us to see the opportunities to participate in your kingdom work and invite others to live with joy.

Add your prayer in your own words.

Amen.

Put It into Practice

This week, see if there is a relationship that needs to be strengthened or restored. It could be in your family or among your friends. Look for ways that God can use hospitality to help bring wholeness.

Take-away Treasure

God reminds us that love is not a sprint but a marathon, and Jesus gives us an example of inexhaustible hospitality. As you plan your week and make plans for the future, remember to make a place in your home and heart to keep on welcoming in his name.

Notes / Prayer Requests

Notes / Prayer Requests

Leader's Guide

Welcome. Relax. Make yourself at home. As the leader of
this study exploring the spiritual practice of Hospitality, you
have the opportunity to create a dynamic experience that
will help your group develop and demonstrate the truths
they are learning. Putting the discipline into practice during
the course of your time together will be an important part
of the journey and make a lasting impact in one another's
lives. Don't wait until everything is just right. Just begin
with what you have, right where you are. Let's start!

Thoughts on Where to Meet

- If you have the chance, encourage each group mem-
  ber to host a gathering. But make sure your host
  knows that you don't expect fresh baked scones from
  scratch or white-glove-test-worthy surroundings.
  Set the tone for a relaxed and open atmosphere with
  a warm welcome wherever you can meet. The host
  can provide the space and the guests can provide the
  goodies. This way you can practice giving and receiving hospitality.

- If you can't meet in homes, consider taking at least one of your meetings on the road. Can you meet at a local place where people from your community gather? A park or a coffee shop or other public space, perhaps.

- If you meet in a church space, consider partnering with another local church group and taking turns hosting. How can you extend your welcome outside your group?

Thoughts on Ways to Foster Welcome

- If many of your members have a hard time meeting due to circumstances, look for ways to work around it. Consider providing childcare if there are moms who have difficulty attending, or meet in an accessible space if someone who might want to join has a disability. Does a morning time work better? Could you meet as smaller groups and then get together as a larger group for an event? Be flexible and see how you can accommodate the needs of the group. Think about what obstacles keep us from practicing and receiving hospitality. Then overcome.

- Incorporate "get to know you" activities to promote sharing. Don't take yourselves too seriously. Let your humor shine through.

Incorporating Other Practices

- *Lift your voices.* Integrate worship throughout the study. Find songs that speak about welcome (some have been included).

- *Commit to lift each other up in prayer.* You may want to have a prayer walk as part of seeing opportunities to serve in your community, or prayer partners who might be able to meet at other times.

- *Dig deep into the word.* Take the study at your own pace but consider including passages for participants to read in between meetings. The *Everyday Matters Bible for Women* has a wealth of additional resources.

- *Pleasures of simplicity.* Take a life inventory of time and stuff to see if anything is getting in the way of a truly full life or find ways to repurpose an abundance of stuff.

- *Give thanks.* Gratitude reenergizes us for humble service. Assemble a group list of one hundred reasons to give thanks.

Ideas for Hospitality

- Assess the needs and opportunities in your community. Connect with a local soup kitchen, youth program, adult day care center, nursing home, or prison ministry.

- Throw a party for adoptive or foster care families, military spouses, or people who are new to your area.

Follow Up

Stay in touch with your fellow study participants and see how you can encourage one another along your journey.

One Last Thing

This study doesn't have to end with the last chapter. Take the opportunity to put together all that you have learned and plan one more gathering to practice hospitality and to welcome others. Think about and prepare the "who, what, when, and where." The study will fill in the "why" and "how." Get the word out. Then make it happen, giving God the thanks and praise.

EVERYDAY MATTERS BIBLE STUDIES
for women

Spiritual practices for everyday life

Acceptance	Mentoring
Bible Study & Meditation	Outreach
Celebration	Prayer
Community	Reconciliation
Confession	Sabbath & Rest
Contemplation	Service
Faith	Silence
Fasting	Simplicity
Forgiveness	Solitude
Gratitude	Stewardship
Hospitality	Submission
Justice	Worship

HENDRICKSON
PUBLISHERS

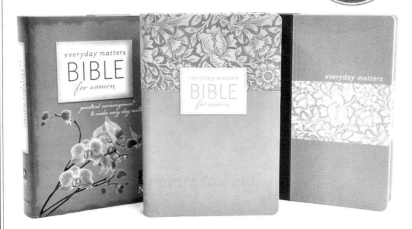